Short Stories for Students, Volume 26

Project Editor: Ira Mark Milne Rights Acquisition and Management: Vernon English, Kelly Quin, Sara Teller, Jhanay Williams Composition: Evi Abou-El-Seoud Manufacturing: Drew Kalasky

Imaging: Lezlie Light

Product Design: Pamela A. E. Galbreath, Jennifer Wahi Content Conversion: Civie Green, Katrina Coach Product Manager: Meggin Condino © 2008 Gale, Cengage Learning ALL RIGHTS RESERVED. No part of this work covered by the copyright herein may be reproduced, transmitted, stored, or used in any form or by any means graphic, electronic, or mechanical, including but not limited to photocopying, recording, scanning, digitizing, taping, Web distribution, information networks, or information storage and retrieval systems, except as permitted under Section 107 or 108 of the 1976 United States Copyright Act, without the prior written permission of the publisher.

Since this page cannot legibly accommodate all copyright notices, the acknowledgments constitute an extension of the copyright notice.

For product information and technology assistance, contact us at **Gale Customer Support, 1-800-877-4253.**

For permission to use material from this text or product, submit all requests online at **www.cengage.com/permissions.**

Further permissions questions can be emailed to **permissionrequest@cengage.com** While every effort has been made to ensure the reliability of the information presented in this publication, Gale, a part of Cengage Learning, does not guarantee the accuracy of the data contained herein. Gale accepts no payment for listing; and inclusion in the publication of any organization, agency, institution, publication, service, or individual does not imply endorsement of the editors or publisher. Errors brought to the attention of the publisher and verified to the satisfaction of the publisher will be corrected in future editions.

Gale
27500 Drake Rd.
Farmington Hills, MI, 48331-3535

ISBN-13: 978-0-7876-8904-9
ISBN-10: 0-7876-8904-1

ISSN 1092-7735

This title is also available as an e-book.

ISBN-13: 978-1-4144-4957-9
ISBN-10: 1-4144-4957-7
Contact your Gale, a part of Cengage Learning sales representative for ordering information.

Printed in the United States of America
1 2 3 4 5 6 7 12 11 10 09 08

Soldier's Home

Ernest Hemingway

1925

Introduction

Ernest Hemingway wrote "Soldier's Home" in 1924 while he was living in Paris with his wife (at the time) Hadley Richardson. The story was first published in 1925 in *Contact Collection of Contemporary Writers*, an anthology that included works by such important writers as Ford Madox Ford, James Joyce, Gertrude Stein, and Ezra Pound, before appearing in Hemingway's exceptional first short story collection, *In Our Time*. The expatriate literary community living in Paris embraced Hemingway, and both Pound and Stein contributed greatly to his growth as a writer. They saw in his work a dramatic shift from earlier literary conventions.

Hemingway himself considered "Soldier's Home" one of his best stories. Indeed, although Hemingway wrote many novels and short stories throughout his life, his early stories, collected in such volumes as *In Our Time* and *Men without Women* (1927), continue to intrigue contemporary critics. Many critics and readers believe the stories in these collections to be Hemingway's finest work. Certainly, "Soldier's Home" and the rest of the stories in *In Our Time* continue to be an important part of the Hemingway canon. The book has remained in print for three-quarters of a century; the most recent edition was published by Scribner in 2003 as a paperback.

The story is a deceptively simple one, detailing the return of a young World War I veteran to his home in a small town in Oklahoma. At the same time, "Soldier's Home" is a finely nuanced work, a story that moves forward, paradoxically, more through what Hemingway does *not* include than through what he does. With characteristic brevity, Hemingway reveals the complex relationship between the protagonist and his mother, the alienation of a young soldier from his culture, and the nearly overpowering sense of loss and lethargy experienced by a generation of young people damaged by the War.

Author Biography

Ernest Hemingway was born on July 21, 1899, in Oak Park, Illinois. His father, Clarence Hemingway, was a doctor, and his mother, Grace Hemingway, was a musician who became a mother and homemaker. Ernest was one of six children.

As a child, Hemingway spent summers at the summer house, Windemere, located on Walloon Lake in northern Michigan. His father taught him to hunt and fish, two passions he pursued for the rest of his life. The natural world became an important influence on Hemingway's later work.

Hemingway graduated from high school in 1917 and went to work as a reporter. The abbreviated style he learned as a reporter would later distinguish his fiction. In 1918, Hemingway joined the American Red Cross against the wishes of his parents to go to the European theater of World War I. Hemingway was assigned to an ambulance unit in Italy. The nineteen-year-old helped to collect body fragments from a munitions explosion, and a few weeks later, found himself under fire while delivering chocolate and cigarettes to Italian troops. His legs were seriously injured, and he was eventually transported to an American Red Cross hospital in Milan. He was to remain there for three months, during which time he endured several surgeries to remove shrapnel from his leg. He also fell in love with his nurse, Agnes von

Kurowsky.

Hemingway returned to the United States after he was well, and expected that Agnes would join him to be wed. She, however, broke off the relationship. Hemingway was deeply wounded by this rejection. Many critics suggest that his return home and the hurt he suffered at Kurowsky's hands form the basis of "Soldier's Home."

Hemingway returned to his work as a reporter, and married Hadley Richardson in 1921. The couple moved to Paris where they became a part of the literary expatriate community. The writer Gertrude Stein famously dubbed the large group of young English-speaking writers in Paris the "Lost Generation."

Through his friendships with poet Ezra Pound and with Stein, Hemingway honed the style for which he would become famous. In 1923, Hemingway published his first collection of writing, *Three Stories and Ten Poems*, which included what might be Hemingway's very first story, "Up in Michigan." The following year found Hemingway assisting Ford Madox Ford with the *transatlantic review*, and bringing out a small volume of vignettes titled *in our time*, not to be confused with his 1925 publication of *In Our Time*, the collection including "Soldier's Home." Hemingway met F. Scott Fitzgerald in 1925 as well, and this association proved fruitful for both writers. In 1926, Hemingway published his first, and arguably his best, novel, *The Sun Also Rises*.

In 1927, Hemingway and Richardson divorced, and he married Pauline Pfieffer. With the success of his novel *The Sun Also Rises* (1926), and a second collection of short stories, *Men without Women* (1927), Hemingway grew increasingly famous. During this period, he also began living the life so identified with him: the big-game-hunting, bull-running life of a man's man. In 1928, at his home in Cuba, Hemingway received word that his father had killed himself.

During World War II, Hemingway scouted for German submarines in the Caribbean and covered the Spanish Civil War, a conflict he wrote about in his 1940 novel, *For Whom the Bell Tolls*. He and his third wife, Martha Gellhorn, divorced in 1946, and Hemingway married Mary Welsh that same year. In 1952, Hemingway published the *Old Man and the Sea*, a novel that was the Pulitzer Prize winner in 1953. The following year, Hemingway received the most important international award for literature, the Nobel Prize.

In 1961, like his father before him, Hemingway took his own life with a shotgun at his home in Ketchum, Idaho. Biographers speculate that the constant pain Hemingway endured from his old wounds and his inherited tendency to depression led to his suicide. At his death, Hemingway was one of the most famous literary figures in the world. His work continues to intrigue critics and readers alike.

Plot Summary

"Soldier's Home" is located at the center of the collection *In Our Time*. Its location, as well as its subject matter, suggests that it is also central to Hemingway's experience of life in the year of its writing, 1924. The story opens with a description of a photograph of Harold Krebs, a young man who had been attending a Methodist college in Kansas before enlisting in the Marines to fight in World War I. This opening snapshot is in stark contrast to the alienated, silent young man Krebs becomes after the war.

Although the war ends in 1918, Krebs does not return home until 1919, the year of the story's setting. Krebs's return is not marked by the parades and accolades given the young men who returned earlier; instead, Krebs discovers that people really do not want to hear about the war unless he exaggerates and lies about his own participation in battle. These lies and erroneous attributions of heroism cause Krebs deep discomfort and nausea. He is unable to speak the truth because no one will listen, and unable to lie because of nausea. In time, he retreats into near silence.

Once home, Krebs fills his days with sleeping, playing pool and practicing the clarinet. He also likes watching the young girls in town from the safety of his own front porch. However, when he is in town, he does not like seeing them. Krebs seems to be isolating himself from all other young people and from life. Although he would like to have a girl, he does not want to talk to women. Again, Krebs demonstrates lethargy and ennui; his alienation from his family, his home, and his culture seem paralyzing.

Krebs wants to "live along without consequences." It is not clear from the text what consequences he is trying to avoid; the implication is that a previous relationship with a woman led to unpleasant consequences, but this remains unspecified. It does, however, point to a general unwillingness on Krebs's part to commit to anything. He does not want to talk to girls, largely because he does not want to tell any more lies. Apparently for Krebs, talking to girls, then, must necessarily include lying.

Media Adaptations

- "Soldier's Home" was released as a

film in 1977 by the Public Broadcasting Service. It was directed by Robert Young and stars Richard Bakus and Nancy March and. In 2006, it became available on DVD.

Krebs begins reading books about the war. From these books, he finally learns something about the war, although he wishes there were more maps. It is puzzling for the reader to understand why books about the war make Krebs feel good, when his own experiences of the war make him feel so uncomfortable. It is as if reading about the War allows him to control the experience in a way that talking about the War does not.

The story comes to a climax one morning when Mrs. Krebs enters her son's bedroom and sits on his bed. She tells him that Mr. Krebs has agreed to let Harold take out the car in the evenings, something he had not allowed before the War. Krebs is not fully awake, but is rude to his mother, suggesting that the only reason his father has offered the car is because his mother has "made him" do so. His mother ignores the remark, and asks Krebs to come downstairs for breakfast.

The scene that follows is both difficult and uncomfortable. When Krebs begins reading the newspaper at the breakfast table, clearly trying to distance himself from his mother, she berates him about his tendency to "muss up" the paper. She treats her son as if he is a child, not a man home from war. Krebs has a pleasant conversation with his sister Helen, whom he says that he loves. When Mrs. Krebs enters the dining room with breakfast, however, she tells Helen to leave because she wants to talk to her son.

Mrs. Krebs asks Krebs what he intends to do with his life. She confronts him with what other young men in their community are already doing. She even asserts, despite Krebs's denial, that everyone is part of God's Kingdom. Mrs. Krebs encourages her son to start going out with girls, and she tells him that she is praying for him. Throughout the lecture, Krebs remains silent, looking at the "bacon fat hardening on the plate." His mother delivers a message from his father: Krebs must visit him in his office on this day. She concludes by asking: "Don't you love your mother, dear boy?"

Krebs responds that he does not love anybody, a response that starts his mother crying and begins the guilt process for Krebs. When she tells him that she held him as a little baby, he replies, sounding like a child: "I know, Mummy. ... I'll try and be a good boy for you." The transformation is painful for reader and character alike. Krebs has been manipulated by his mother to the point where he even kneels with her while she prays.

The story concludes with Krebs leaving the house, thinking he will go to Kansas City to get a job. There is no indication, however, that he does so. Readers must draw their own conclusion as to

Krebs's future, because Hemingway leaves the door open to speculation.

Characters

Harold Krebs

Harold Krebs is a young man who has recently returned from his service with the U.S. Marines during World War I. His home is in a small town in Oklahoma. The story opens with the description of two photographs: in the first, Krebs is pictured with his fraternity brothers at the Methodist college he attended before the war. He is dressed exactly like the other young men and seems to have a place among them. In the second photograph, he is pictured with another soldier and some German girls immediately after the war in Europe. He is pictured here as being too big for his uniform, suggesting that he does not fit comfortably into either his uniform or his life. Now, with his return to Oklahoma, he seems to belong nowhere.

Krebs did not receive a hero's welcome on his return because he arrived after the other veterans. While the text of the story stipulates that Krebs arrived "years" after the other soldiers, this description could be ironic, since it is a historical fact that the Marine Corps unit of which Krebs was a part came back to the United States in 1919, just one year after the end of the war.

In the month since his return, Krebs has done little more than sleep, play pool, and sit on his front porch watching girls. He has little interest in anything else, and appears completely disengaged from his family, save for his younger sister Helen, with whom he seems to have a loving relationship. Krebs's relationship with his mother is particularly problematic. When she begins to nag him about deciding what he wants to do with his life, Krebs tells her that he does not love her. The remark seems to devastate Mrs. Krebs, and Krebs quickly tries to make up for it.

Several critics, such as Arthur Waldhorn in *A Reader's Guide to Ernest Hemingway* (1972) connect Krebs with Nick Adams, the protagonist in several other stories of *In Our Time*. Others, such as Kenneth Lynn in his book *Hemingway,* assert that Krebs is an autobiographical character and that his relationship with his mother stems from Hemingway's own troubled relationship with his mother. Still others, such as Thomas Putman, see in Krebs a representative of the returned war victim, unable to reconnect with his family. Hemingway's understated characterization makes each of these interpretations a possibility.

Helen Krebs

Helen Krebs is Harold Krebs's younger sister. She plays "indoor," the term used for women's baseball. Her role in the story is as a foil to Mrs. Krebs. Helen adores her brother, and sees him as a hero. She demands no explanations nor stories. Krebs is able to be honest with her, and she with him. Although she appears only briefly in the story, she is also a contrast to all of the girls that Krebs watches from the front porch. She is unlike the girls who demand talk and who present consequences. Finally, Helen Krebs is the only character in the story with whom Harold Krebs seems to have a loving relationship. There is a slight hint that the relationship is unseemly; Helen calls Harold her "beau" and Harold does not object. On the other hand, the exchange seems nonetheless innocent. In the last line of the story, Krebs decides that he will go to the school to watch Helen play indoor baseball. This tenuous thread of connection with another member of his family offers hope that Krebs will one day truly find his way home.

Mr. Krebs

An important character in this story paradoxically never appears. Harold Krebs's father does not step into the story at any time except through messages that are conveyed through Mrs. Krebs. A telling phrase, "Mr. Krebs was noncommittal," describes the elder Krebs's absence from the story. There is the sense that Harold is merely following in his father's footsteps, absenting himself from all conflict, discussion, and commitment. When Mr. Krebs sends word through Mrs. Krebs that Harold should come and see him, Harold ignores the request. He appears to hold his father in disdain for his inability to stand up to his wife. Oddly, it is in his absence that Mr. Krebs reveals the most about the dysfunction of this family.

From the text of the story, it would be possible to arrive at two very different understandings of Mr. Krebs. On the one hand, the fact that he only sends messages through his wife, including one that orders Krebs to visit his father's office, could suggest that he is a tyrannical figure who sees himself above the other members of his family. Like a general, he sends his orders through his underlings. On the other hand—and this is the more widely accepted interpretation of Mr. Krebs—he is seen as a weak character, dominated by his wife. Krebs's disdain for his father and his disregard for his father's orders seem to support this interpretation. In addition, critics who read this story as autobiographical point to Mr. and Mrs. Hemingway as models for Mr. and Mrs. Krebs. By all accounts, Hemingway found his mother to be controlling and the dominant partner of the marriage. While relying too heavily on biographical detail to build an interpretation of a story can produce readings that are not in concert with the story, it is nevertheless interesting to speculate how much Hemingway's mother influenced her son's portrait of this marriage.

Mrs. Krebs

Mrs. Krebs is Harold's mother. She is a pious woman who appears to rule her household. She uses her husband's absence to manipulate those around her by phrasing her requests as messages from Mr. Krebs. Mrs. Krebs seems unable to accept the fact that Krebs has changed, and that he is no longer her little boy. Often, she goes into Krebs's room while he is lying in bed and sits on the bed talking to him. Her conversation usually centers around what other young men in the town are doing with their lives, and the implication is that Krebs must decide quickly what he is going to do. She often asks Krebs about the War, but fails to listen to his responses. It is as if she does not want to hear anything unpleasant, or anything that might suggest that the War has somehow changed Krebs. A change in Krebs might suggest that he is no longer her little boy, and that she might not have control of him any longer. Mrs. Krebs precipitates the climactic scene in the book at the breakfast table when she confronts Krebs about getting a job. When she asks: "Don't you love your mother, dear boy?" Krebs responds that he does not, and that he does not love anyone. This brings his mother to tears. She tells him that when he was a baby, she held him next to her heart. This image nauseates Krebs. It is difficult to determine whether the nausea is caused by the lies he tells his mother to keep her from crying, or if the image of being held to her breast is deeply disturbing to Krebs. In any event, with her tears, Mrs. Krebs succeeds in reducing Krebs to a childlike version of himself: "I know, Mummy," he says, "I'll try and be a good boy for you." While Krebs might have been a powerful soldier in the War, this scene illustrates that it is Mrs. Krebs who holds the power in the family.

Sister

In this very brief story, there is one additional character who never makes it into the text except for one very brief mention. Krebs has two sisters. Helen has dialogue and Krebs reports that she is his favorite sister. The second sister is never named nor does the story provide any text to describe her. While it might at first glance seem an unimportant detail, her absence from the story serves to emphasize the alienation Krebs feels from his family. His second sister's life is so unimportant to Krebs that he never thinks of her nor does she figure in any consideration of his life.

Themes

Alienation

In "Soldier's Home," Hemingway introduces yet another of his young male characters who seems lost and alone in the world. Joseph DeFalco writes in *The Hero in Hemingway's Short Stories* that "the central character of the story is Krebs, and he is the personification of man alienated from the traditional source of solace. Church, family, and society no longer command allegiance from the individual who has experienced the purgatorial initiation of war."

To be alienated means to become an alien, a word that ultimately derives from the Latin word, *alius*, meaning "another." The word alias also comes from this root, and also carries with it the connotation of the division of identity. Someone using an alias, for example, is pretending to be someone he or she is not. An alien is also someone who is not a citizen of the particular country in which he or she lives, or someone who is excluded. In popular culture, the word alien often is used to refer to a being from outer space.

Certainly, it is unlikely that even a being from outer space would find itself more alienated than Krebs finds himself in his home town. This is, of course, ironic: home is supposed to be where the heart is, but Krebs is unable to locate his, or any other heart, in his small Oklahoma town. He moves through the story like a man in a dream, unable to shake lose from his stupor.

What causes Krebs's alienation? This is a question that elicits some debate. Clearly, one explanation is that Krebs suffers from what was called "shell shock" during World War I. Today, the term to describe the aftereffects of violence and death on witnesses is post traumatic stress disorder, or PTSD. The horrors—and the excitement—of war can make the return home very difficult for the veteran.

Topics for Further Study

- Research the writers living in Paris during the early 1920's, including F. Scott Fitzgerald, Gertrude Stein, James Joyce, Ezra Pound, and Ford Madox Ford. What was their relationship to Ernest Hemingway? How did the interactions between these important writers influence their writing? Give a class presentation on your findings.

- Reviewer Paul Rosenfeld, in a 1925 article appearing in the *New Republic*, called Hemingway a "Cubist" writer. Visit an art gallery or use the Internet to view several Cubist paintings. Write an essay in which you explore how these works of art are like or unlike Hemingway's stories in *In Our Time*.

- Read Tim O'Brien's *The Things They Carried*, a book many critics believe to be the best writing about the Vietnam War ever produced. Compare and contrast O'Brien's style and structure with Hemingway's writing in *In Our Time*. In particular, make a graph in which you compare and contrast the character Norman Bowker from O'Brien's short story "Speaking of Courage" with Harold Krebs in "Soldier's Home."

- Read several biographical accounts of Hemingway's life. Write an essay in which you explain why critics choose to read "Soldier's Home" as a semi-autobiographical account of Hemingway's return from war?

Another compelling reason for Krebs's alienation is that he is caught in a world that is reeling wildly toward the modern era. Although many credit World War I with the rapid changes the world endured in the early twentieth century, in truth the transition from nineteenth century morals, culture, and belief systems had begun before the old century was even over. In virtually every field of human knowledge, change was rampant. In 1905, Einstein announced the special theory of relativity, a theory that shook the very underpinnings of our understanding of physical matter. In 1907, Picasso painted "Les Desmoiselles d'Avignon," a painting of prostitutes that stretched the possibilities of artistic representation to the breaking point. In 1920, just five years before the writing of "Soldier's Home," women in the United States were first given the right to vote. Everything changed, from the inside out and from the ground up. Krebs truly is an alien, a stranger in a strangely modern land that changed in the few short years he was away.

Commitment and Consequences

"Soldier's Home" is also a story about the main character's inability to make commitments for fear of the consequences those commitments might engender. It is unclear from the story why he has these fears; no mention is made of previous involvements that have turned sour. It is true, however, that the most extended discussion of commitment and consequences occurs when Krebs considers the girls of his hometown. Although he likes to watch the girls, he seems to feel that it will be too much effort to commit: "When he was in town, their appeal to him was not very strong. ... He did not want themselves really. They were too complicated. There was something else. Vaguely he wanted a girl but he did not want to have to work to get her." The "something else" is oddly troubling; it hints that in his previous life, he might have had to work to get a girl, and that somehow this relationship was too difficult to consider now that the War was over.

In addition to his reluctance to committing to getting to know a girl, Krebs also is unwilling to take on the consequences of such a relationship: "He did not want any consequences. He did not want any consequences ever again. He wanted to live along without consequences." Later he states: "He knew he could never get through it all again." These two passages, as well as others in this section, strongly suggest that Krebs has had a relationship with a young woman before the war. In addition, it also suggests that the consequences of the relationship were somehow unpleasant. At the very least, the pleasure of the relationship itself was outweighed by the complications.

The inability to engage emotionally in human relationships is a theme that Hemingway develops in this story through the issue of commitment and consequences; it is a theme that he returns to again in his later novels. Most writers agree that this characteristic theme is particularly compelling; John

Pidgeon, however, writing in *Modern Times*, argues that Hemingway "had only one tune to play. It is the theme of non-commitment and uninvolvement. This is a nihilistic idea and does not in the end qualify him for the honor of literary genius." What Pidgeon misses, of course, is that Hemingway himself took very seriously his commitment to his readers, and that Krebs's non-involvement is not Hemingway's.

Krebs's lack of emotional commitment has one important exception in the story. He loves his younger sister. If there is any hope in this story, it resides in this relationship. While Krebs might desire of life of no consequence, it is at least possible that Helen will pull him back into his life.

Style

Changing Narrative Voice

One of Hemingway's most characteristic stylistic features is the narrative voice that tells his stories. This feature is particularly interesting in "Soldier's Home" in that although the sentence structure and vocabulary remain consistent throughout the novel, the voice itself changes from the beginning to end, starting from what would appear to be an objective, omniscient, third person point of view to a highly subjective, nearly first person internal narrative.

Many critics have commented on Hemingway's narrative style. Thomas Strychacz, writing in the *Cambridge Companion to Ernest Hemingway*, for example, argues that the narrative voice is a remarkable artistic achievement in "Soldier's Home." "Understanding Krebs'[s] behavior depends in part on how we read Hemingway's striking stylistic performance. ... Krebs'[s] homecoming is rendered with obsessive repetitiveness in a flat prose so neutral that it sounds almost scientifically detached."

The narration in the beginning of the story seems nearly voiceless; there are a series of declarative statements describing in flat detail two different photographs of Krebs. The narrative is detached from that which it describes, looking in from the outside. By the fourth paragraph, however, there is a shift. The sentences become longer, and begin to describe what goes on inside of Krebs:

> A distaste for everything that had happened to him in the war set in because of the lies he had told. All of the times that had been able to make him feel cool and clear inside himself when he thought of them; the times so long back when he had done the one thing, the only thing for a man to do, easily and naturally, when he might have done something else, now lost their cool, valuable quality and then were lost themselves.

Because the prose is so elliptical, that is, because the narrative leaves so much out, it becomes closer to the interior monologues, or stream of consciousness writing of other modernists, such as Virginia Woolfe or James Joyce. The narrative voice is clearly sympathetic to Krebs. As it follows him through his day, there is never any negative judgment of his choices to stay in bed or play pool or just watch girls walk by. When Krebs's mother begins her diatribe about finding work, the narrative voice reports what she says in a seemingly objective way, but also links her voice to "the bacon fat hardening on his plate," a particularly unattractive image. Further, by the end of the story, the narrative voice seems to have merged with that of Krebs himself. Seven sentences in the last paragraph start with the word "he" and could just as well start with "I."

As a technique, shifting the narrative in this way leads the reader from an objective assessment of Krebs to an identification with him, troubled by what he has seen in the war, lost in the new world called home, and berated by a mother who loves him but no longer knows him.

Imperative Dialogue

If the narrative voice of "Soldier's Home" is the first of Hemingway's characteristic stylistic devices, then surely dialogue is the second. Robert Paul Lamb, writing in *Twentieth Century Literature*, argues that in stories like "Soldier's Home" and "Hills Like White Elephants," "Hemingway evolved the techniques that would change the nature of twentieth-century fictional dialogue." As Lamb notes, Hemingway's technique included stripping dialogue to its barest by omitting all but the most necessary words. At the same time, Hemingway relied on the dialogue to carry the weight of the story.

"Soldier's Home" does not have the amount of dialogue present in several of Hemingway's other stories; nonetheless, the dialogue carries considerable weight in the construction of character in this story. The character with the most words in "Soldier's Home" is not the protagonist, but rather it is his mother. For a character in a Hemingway short story, Mrs. Krebs talks a lot; not only does she have more speeches, her lines are longer than those of any other character. Analyzing her lines, it is possible to deduce that her favorite mode of speech is the imperative mode. She tells Krebs not to muss the paper, to put down the paper, not to look the way he looks, to make a start at something, and to pray. In addition, she makes additional commands, thinly veiled as questions. For example, she says: "Have you decided what you are going to do yet, Harold?" This is not truly a question, but rather a statement that Harold must decide what to do. Likewise, when she asks Krebs: "Would you kneel and pray with me, Harold?", she is not interested at all in what Harold would like. Rather, this is a command made explicit three lines later: "Now, you pray, Harold."

Furthermore, Mrs. Krebs has more speeches and more words than any other character in the story at least partially because she speaks for her husband. More than half of her statements refer to her husband, or report things that her husband has supposedly said. Ironically, her speeches have erased the husband from the story. He never actually appears, as he has been effectively silenced by his wife. Likewise, Mrs. Krebs appears to be attempting the same linguistic maneuver with her son. The more that she talks, the less Harold talks. By the end of the story, readers are left with the impression that Harold might walk right out of his house, silenced by his mother, on his way to Kansas City.

Historical Context

World War I

World War I, fought between 1914 and 1918, engulfed Europe in some of the most terrible fighting ever experienced by humankind. To this day, the trenches of the Western Front evoke horror among scholars and students alike. When the United States entered the War in 1917, on the side of the British and the French, the fresh troops turned the tide for the Allied forces. At the same time, young American men were subjected to unbelievably brutal conditions. Many Americans suffered from what was then called shell shock, and has since become known as post traumatic stress disorder (PTSD).

Hemingway himself did not serve in the trenches, but rather was posted to Italy. That he has chosen, however, to place Krebs's service on the Western Front of France and Belgium in some of the most brutal battles of the war is highly significant. In the third paragraph, he states that Krebs "had been at Belleau Wood, Soissons, the Champagne, St. Miheil and in the Argonne." These were real battles that the Marines participated in, and Hemingway's readers would certainly have recognized these names. The new technology of war, including machine guns, mustard gas, and aerial bombardment, tied with outmoded military strategy led to an extraordinarily high casualty count in each of these battles.

Reading "Soldier's Home" without an understanding of this backdrop leads to an incomplete understanding of Krebs's complete incapacitation. His war experience, like that of men before him and men after him, becomes the pivotal focus in his life.

The Lost Generation

In the years immediately after World War I, there was very rapid social change in the United States. Technology and the economy boomed, and women achieved greater freedom, receiving the right to vote in 1920. As Krebs notices as he watches the girls while he sits on the front porch, they wore their skirts and their hair shorter than they had before he left.

As American soldiers made their way home, some found it difficult to settle back into their prewar lives. For some, particularly those with literary aspirations, the strong U.S. dollar made it possible for them to return to Europe where they could live for much less than in the United States. In addition, they were familiar with the language and they appreciated less restrictive moral codes. Between 1921 and 1924, the American population of Paris grew from 6,000 to 30,000.

Compare & Contrast

- **1920s:** The members of the American Expeditionary Force have returned from Europe to find a very different country awaiting them. Shocked by the horrors of the war, and exposed to the world at large, some men have a difficult time settling back into life in their home towns.

  Today: The members of the United States Armed Forces cycle in and out of the war in Iraq, leaving their families and loved ones. Men and women serving in Iraq may have difficulty readjusting to life back at home.

- **1920s:** A large group of American writers live in Paris, enjoying the low cost of living, the unrestrictive moral codes, and the vibrant cultural life.

  Today: Although there are Americans living in Paris, there is no longer an American writers' colony of the size or prestige of earlier days.

- **1920s:** The literary and artistic avant-garde experiment with genre and convention. They push the boundaries of representational art and abstraction.

Today: The experimentation in art and literature begun almost a century earlier continues into the twenty-first century. New technologies greatly expand the limit of what is possible in graphic arts and written texts.

By 1924, the year Hemingway wrote "Soldier's Home," the large community of expatriate writers included such literary luminaries as F. Scott Fitzgerald, Ezra Pound, Gertrude Stein, and James Joyce. Hemingway found his way to this community through a letter of introduction to Stein, written for him by American writer Sherwood Anderson.

Gertrude Stein famously coined the phrase "The Lost Generation" to describe this large group of young writers that frequented her literary salon. Hemingway picked up on the phrase, using it as an epigraph for his memoir of the Paris years called *The Moveable Feast*, and he also used the idea of a lost generation, a generation damaged by war and violence, unable to commit or put down roots in many of his stories and novels of the period. Disillusioned by the war, the lost generation rejected the morality of their parents, believing the values they grew up with were a sham. Krebs's difficulty with his parents, and his discomfort with his mother's piety, identify him as a member of this generation.

Critical Overview

In Our Time, Hemingway's groundbreaking collection of short stories, appeared in 1925 to extensive critical review. In many ways, this book was as revolutionary in literature as Picasso's early Cubist work had been in art. (Cubism was a highly influential art form that emerged early in the twentieth century. Cubists such as Picasso broke an object into pieces, analyzed the object, and then reassembled the object in an abstract form in an attempt to offer alternative perspectives of the object.) In a critique appearing in the *New Republic* shortly after the book's publication, Paul Rosenfeld writes: "Hemingway's short stories belong with Cubist painting, 'Le Sacre du Printemps' and other recent work bringing a feeling of positive forces through primitive modern idiom." It should be noted, however, that by 2006, critics such as Lisa Narbeshuber, having arrived at a different analysis of Cubism, argue that "Soldier's Home" and the stories of *In Our Time* stand in stark contrast to the ideals of Cubism. As Narbeshuber writes in the *Hemingway Review*, "Behind the spirit of the original Cubists working between 1907 and 1914, when Cubism was a unique way of seeing the world, rather than just a set of techniques, is an attitude towards reality that Hemingway decidedly rejects."

In any event, the book was so different from a traditional collection of short stories that contemporary critics had a difficult time even knowing how to classify it. The famous English novelist D. H. Lawrence, writing in 1927 in *Calendar of Modern Letters*, for example, suggests that "*In Our Time* calls itself a book of stories, but it isn't that. It is a series of successive sketches from a man's life and makes a fragmentary novel."

Not all critics appreciated Hemingway's style. In a famous essay included in *Life and Letters*, Wyndham Lewis, the English painter and writer, takes exception to American writer Gertrude Stein's influence on the young Hemingway, particularly in "Soldier's Home." He writes: "There is no possibility, I am afraid, of slurring over this. It is just a thing you have to accept as an unfortunate handicap in an artist who is in some respects above praise…. Krebs, for instance, is a full-blooded example of Hemingway [Gertrude] steining away for all he is worth."

"Soldier's Home," along with the "Nick Adams" stories, is frequently singled out from the collection for critical commentary. In 1963, Joseph DeFalco presented what continues to be one of the most important readings of the short story, and this is included in his book *The Hero in Hemingway's Short Stories*. He offers an analysis of the narrative structure of the story, arguing that this structure parallels Krebs's process of individuation. He further asserts that "the root of Krebs's conflict is grounded in the home environment." Further, critics John J. McKenna and David Raabe see Krebs's problems to be rooted in temperamental conflicts with his parents. They write in *Studies in Short Fiction* that "Hemingway's 'Soldier's Home' is a remarkable illustration of the conflict and tension that result from the collision of different core values arising from contrasting temperaments."

Another group of critics, while agreeing that "Soldier's Home" is autobiographical in that it reflects Hemingway's experiences, choose instead to focus on the theme of the soldier returning from war. Matthew C. Stewart, writing in *Papers on Language & Literature*, for example, asserts: "Clearly mother-son dynamics are of great importance in "Soldier's Home," but the story's *sine qua non* is the depiction of a war veteran struggling to readjust to post-war civilian life. The family tensions cannot be seen as an issue somehow distinct from Krebs's status as a returned soldier." Likewise, George Cheatham, in the *Hemingway Review*, takes a decidedly historical view of the story, arguing that "increasingly critics have come to realize what Hemingway's title, *In Our Time*, has been declaring all along—that time, place, and cultural history do matter for readers of this Hemingway text." Steven Trout, in another issue of the *Hemingway Review*, also provides a historical rationale for Krebs's conflict by connecting it with the actual problems encountered by the American Expeditionary Forces when they returned after the War.

Still other critics, while arguing that an understanding of Hemingway's real-life war experience as well as that of Krebs is crucial for reading "Soldier's Home," assert that this experience can be generalized to include returning veterans from other conflicts. Vietnam War veterans in particular seem to find an affinity with Krebs's dilemma. Frederic J. Svoboda, writing in *A Historical Guide to Ernest Hemingway* comments:

> Vietnam War veterans have suggested to me that the experience of reading Hemingway's stories is like being dropped behind enemy lines, with everything to be figured out in an instant. These veterans have found the disillusioned World War I veteran Krebs of "Soldier's Home" reflecting accurately their experiences of ambiguous and unsatisfying homecoming.

It is, therefore, not much of a stretch to see Hemingway's influence on later writers of war experience, such as Tim O'Brien, the quintessential author of Vietnam War stories.

In a particularly well-written analysis of the story, Robert Paul Lamb in the *Hemingway Review*, provides not only an excellent overview of the published criticism surrounding "Soldier's Home," he also suggests that the story is like other iconic texts of the early twentieth century such as F. Scott Fitzgerald's *The Great Gatsby*, John Dos Passos's *Manhattan Transfer*, and T. S. Eliot's "The Hollow Men." All attempt, according to Lamb, to capture "the experience of a people in painful transition: their failed institutions, their confused and often tragic attempts to hold onto past ideals and ideologies, and their inevitable failure."

That this small story in a slim volume provokes so many, and often heated, critical discussions is a testament to its power. As readers continue to experience the world in new and different ways, and as war continues to be a part of contemporary reality, it is likely that many more interpretations remain to be written.

What Do I Read Next?

- *A Farewell to Arms* (1929) is Hemingway's important novel about World War I. This novel can be read as a companion piece to the stories in *In Our Time*.
- *The Things They Carried* (1990) is a collection of related short stories by Tim O'Brien, all set during the

Vietnam War. O'Brien's work has often been compared to Hemingway's, and there is a close connection between O'Brien's story "Speaking of Courage" and Hemingway's "Soldier's Home."

- Michael Reynold's *Hemingway: The Paris Years* (1989) is considered to be the benchmark biography about Hemingway's early years as a writer. Reynold's book covers the period immediately before and after the writing of "Soldier's Home."

- Raymond Carver is a twentieth-century American short story writer whose work shows the influence of Hemingway's style. *Where I'm Calling From: New and Selected Stories* (1988) is an interesting book for anyone interested in Hemingway's short stories.

- *Modern Art: Painting, Sculpture, and Architecture* (1992), by Sam Hunter and John Jacobus, provides an excellent overview of modernism and the Cubist revolution. Copious illustrations and photographs of important works of art are included.

- *Ernest Hemingway: A Literary Reference* (2002), edited by Robert W. Trogden, is a documentary history of Hemingway and his writing. Included are facsimiles of Hemingway's manuscripts as well as abundant photographs from all periods of Hemingway's life.

Sources

Cheatham, George, "The World War I Battle of Mons and Hemingway's *In Our Time* Chapter III," in *The Hemingway Review*, Vol. 26, No. 2, p. 44.

DeFalco, Joseph, *The Hero in Hemingway's Short Stories*, University of Pittsburgh Press, 1963, pp. 137-45.

Fish, Stanley, *Self-Consuming Artifacts: The Experience of Seventeenth Century Literature*, University of California Press, 1972.

Hemingway, Ernest, "Soldier's Home," in *In Our Time*, Scribner, 2003, pp. 67-78

Lamb, Robert Paul, "Hemingway and the Creation of Twentieth-Century Dialogue," in *Twentieth Century Literature*, Vol. 42, Winter 1996, pp. 453-80.

———, "The Love Song of Harold Krebs: Form, Argument, and Meaning in Hemingway's 'A Soldier's Home,'" in the *Hemingway Review*, Vol. 14, No. 2, Spring 1995, pp. 18-37.

Lawrence, D. H., Review of *In Our Time*, in *Hemingway: The Critical Heritage*, edited by Jeffrey Meyers, Routledge & Keegan Paul, 1982, p. 75; originally published in *Calendar of Modern Letters*, Vol. 4, April 1927.

Lewis, Wyndham, "Wyndham Lewis on Hemingway," in *Hemingway: The Critical*

Heritage, edited by Jeffrey Meyers, Routledge & Keegan Paul, 1982, pp. 186-209; originally published as "The Dumb Ox: A Study of Ernest Hemingway," in *Life and Letters*, Vol. 10, April 1934.

Lynn, Kenneth, *Hemingway*, Simon and Schuster, 1987, p. 259-60.

Kaplan, Steven, "The Undying Uncertainty of the Narrator in Tim O'Brien's *The Things They Carried*," in *Critique: Studies in Contemporary Fiction*, Vol. 35,No. 1, Fall 1993, pp. 43-53.

McKenna, John J., and David M. Raabe, "Using Temperament Theory to Understand Conflict in Hemingway's 'Soldier's Home,'" in *Studies in Short Fiction*, Vol. 34, No. 2, Spring 1997, pp. 203-13.

Murfin, Ross, and Supryia M. Ray, *The Bedford Glossary of Critical and Literary Terms*, 2nd edition, Bedford/St. Martin's, 2003, pp. 240; 391-97.

Narbeshuber, Lisa, "Hemingway's *In Our Time*: Cubism, Conservation and the Suspension of Identification," in the *Hemingway Review*, Vol. 25, No. 2, Spring 2006, pp. 9-30.

Pidgeon, John A., "Ernest Hemingway," in *Modern Age*, Vol. 48, No. 1, Winter 2006, pp. 90-92.

Putnam, Thomas, "Hemingway on War and Its Aftermath," in *Prologue*, Vol. 38, No. 1, Spring 2006, pp. 22-29.

Rosenfeld, Paul, Review of *In Our Time*, in *Hemingway: The Critical Heritage*, edited by

Jeffrey Meyers, Routledge & Keegan Paul, 1982, p. 67; originally published in *New Republic*, November 25, 1925.

Smith, Paul, Review of "Soldier's Home," in *A Reader's Guide to the Short Stories of Ernest Hemingway*, G. K. Hall, 1989, pp. 68-74.

Stewart, Matthew C., "Ernest Hemingway and World War I: Combatting [sic] Recent Psychobiographical Reassessments, Restoring the War," in *Papers on Language & Literature*, Vol. 36, No. 2, Spring 2000, pp. 198-217.

Strychacz, Thomas, "*In Our Time*, Out of Season," in *The Cambridge Companion to Ernest Hemingway*, edited by Scott Donaldson, Cambridge University Press, 1991, p. 74-75.

Svoboda, Frederic J., "The Great Themes in Hemingway: Love, War, Wilderness, and Loss," in *A Historical Guide to Ernest Hemingway*, edited by Linda Wagner-Martin, Oxford University Press, 2000, pp. 155-72.

Trout, Steven, "'Where Do We Go from Here?' Ernest Hemingway's 'Soldier's Home' and American Veterans of World War I," in the *Hemingway Review*, Vol. 20, No.1, Fall 2000, p. 22-29.

Waldhorn, Arthur, *A Reader's Guide to Ernest Hemingway*, Farrar, Straus, and Giroux, 1972, p. 67.

Zapf, Hubert, "Reflection vs. Daydream: Two Types of the Implied Reader in Hemingway's Fiction," in *New Critical Approaches to the Short*

Stories of Ernest Hemingway, edited by Jackson J. Brenner, Duke University Press, 1990, pp. 96-111.

Further Reading

Cohen, Milton A., *Hemingway's Laboratory: The Paris in Our Time*, University of Alabama Press, 2005.

> This is a close, yet readable study, of Hemingway's *in our time*, the slim volume of vignettes that were incorporated into the later collection, *In Our Time*.

Howard, Michael, *The First World War: A Very Short Introduction*, Oxford University Press, 2007.

> This book provides a useful introduction to the causes and conditions of World War I, providing the necessary context for a reading of Hemingway's early work.

Rovit, Earl, and Gary Brenner, *Ernest Hemingway*, revised edition, Twayne Publishers, 1995.

> Written for students, this text provides a biography, bibliography, and thorough introduction to Hemingway.

Vernon, Alex, *Soldiers Once and Still: Ernest Hemingway, James Salter, and Tim O'Brien*, University of Iowa Press, 2004.

> Vernon provides an excellent analysis of the war literature

produced by three of the twentieth century's best war writers.

CPSIA information can be obtained
at www.ICGtesting.com
Printed in the USA
BVHW041014260721
612868BV00015B/961